Water on Earth

Earth contains 1.4 10^{21} liters (3.7 10^{20} gallons) of water.
200 billion liters (53 billion gallons) for each person.

If earth would be smooth like the surface of a billiard ball and all water would be evenly distributed on the surface, then it would be 2,745 m (9,006 ft) deep.

If all water on earth would be piled up on the United States, the resulting column of water would be 142 km (88 miles) high, reaching up into space.

Florida, during Shuttle Mission STS-95 seen from orbit.
Image: NASA

H$_2$O

Water consists of two Hydrogen and one Oxygen atoms.

Hydrogen is the most abundant element in the universe – all other elements are ultimately created from Hydrogen.

Oxygen is the most common element in the Earth's crust, making up 48.9% of its mass.

99.762% of all terrestrial Oxygen atoms consist of 8 protons and 8 neutrons. The number 8 is considered magic in the Nuclear Shell Model. Oxygen is doubly magic.

Lake in a crater of the Laki volcanic fissure on Iceland. The last eruption in 1783/84 was the largest in the history of mankind. It caused famine in all of Europe, which led to the French Revolution.

Water distribution

97% of all global water is salt water in the oceans. Only 3% is fresh water.

68.7% out of this 3% is concentrated in the ice caps and glaciers. Ground water accounts for 30.1%, surface water only 0.3%. All other contributors sum to 0.9%.

Among the 0.3% surface water, lakes provide the dominating portion with 87% followed by swamps with 11% and rivers with 2%.

The Svartifoss waterfall in Iceland's Skaftafell national park with Basalt pillars.

Oceans

71% of Earth's surface is covered by seas.

There are 5 oceans: Arctic, Atlantic, Indian, Pacific and Southern Ocean.

The legendary seven seas were: Atlantic Ocean, Pacific Ocean, Indian Ocean, Caribbean, Mediterranean, Yellow Sea, North Sea.

The Pacific is the largest Ocean.

The deepest point of all oceans is the 2400 km (1491 miles) long Mariana Trench in the Pacific off the coast of Japan, with a depth off 11,304 m (37,087 ft).

The Pacific Ocean surges against the coast of O'ahu east of Honululu.

Glaciers

Glaciers are defined as a body of ice, created from snow in a clearly defined area. They cover 10% of all land.

The total mass of all glaciers has been shrinking since 1850.

Glacier movement ranges from 150 m/year (492 ft/year) in the Alps to 10 km/year (6.2 miles/year) on Greenland.

The Lambert Glacier in the Antarctic is the largest and longest glacier in the world (420x130 km², 261x81 miles²).
The largest glacier in the US is Gannett Glacier with 3.63 km² (897 acres) in 1999.

The Franz-Josef Glacier on New Zealand's southern island stretches down to 300 meters above sea level.

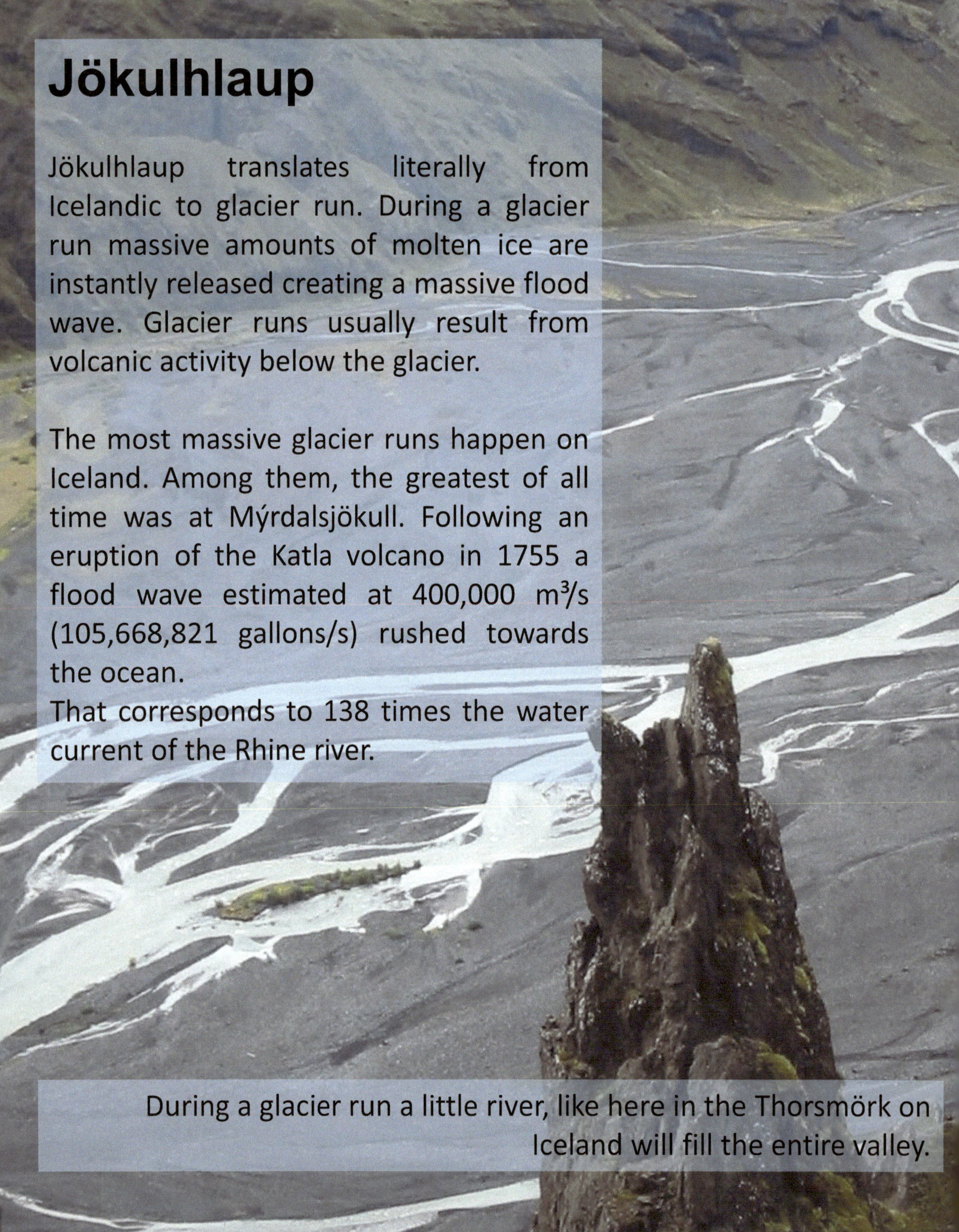

Jökulhlaup

Jökulhlaup translates literally from Icelandic to glacier run. During a glacier run massive amounts of molten ice are instantly released creating a massive flood wave. Glacier runs usually result from volcanic activity below the glacier.

The most massive glacier runs happen on Iceland. Among them, the greatest of all time was at Mýrdalsjökull. Following an eruption of the Katla volcano in 1755 a flood wave estimated at 400,000 m³/s (105,668,821 gallons/s) rushed towards the ocean.
That corresponds to 138 times the water current of the Rhine river.

During a glacier run a little river, like here in the Thorsmörk on Iceland will fill the entire valley.

Lakes

A lake is a body of water which is completely surrounded by land, with the exception of waterways going in and out. The largest lake is the Caspian Sea. (saltwater, surface: 393,898 km² (152,084 miles²).

The largest fresh water lake is Lake Superior (surface: 82,414 km² (31,820 miles²).

Lake Baikal in Russia is not only the deepest lake (depth: up to 1642 m, 5,387 ft) but also contains the most water of all lakes.

The deepest laying lake is the Dead Sea, at 420 m (1,378 ft) below mean sea level.

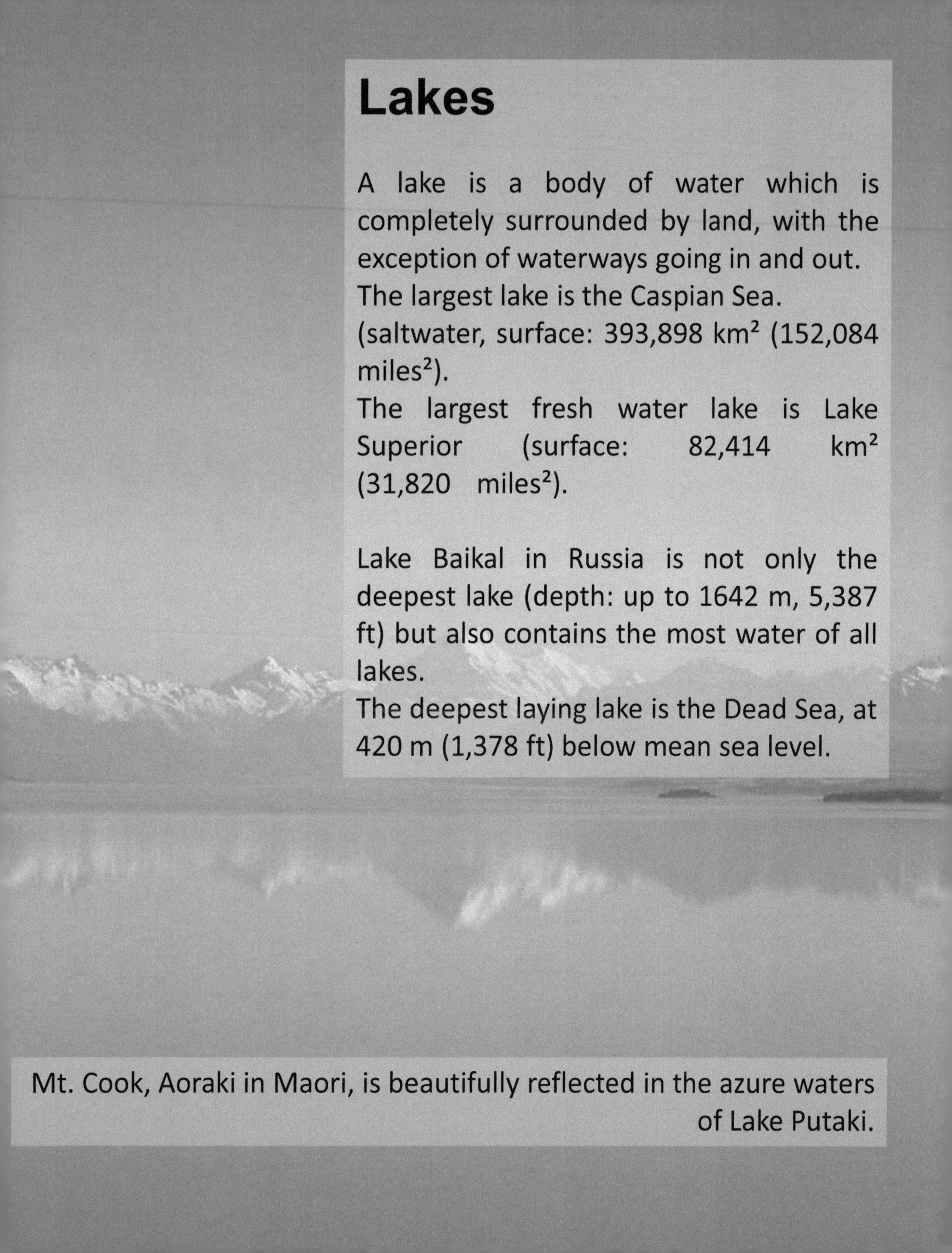

Mt. Cook, Aoraki in Maori, is beautifully reflected in the azure waters of Lake Putaki.

Swamps and Moors

A swamp is a wetland in the vicinity of lakes or rivers.

A moor is a swamp which creates peat at its surface.

Contrary to public opinion the Everglades in Florida are a marsh not a swamp. Marshes are dominated by grass type plants while swamps are dominated by trees.

Pantanal Swamp in Bolivia is the largest swamp on Earth (150,000 km², 37 million acres).
Russia's Wassjugan-Moor is the largest in the world (50,000 km², 12 million acres).

Waterway in Everglades National Park.

Rivers

Rivers are waters flowing over land.

The longest rivers are the Nile (6,670 km, 4,145 miles), Amazon (6,448 km, 4,007 miles), the Jangtsekiang (6,380 km, 3,964 miles) and the Missouri-Mississippi (6,051 km, 3,760 miles).

A water current of 206,000 m³/s (54 million gallons/s) makes the Amazon the fastest flowing river on Earth.

A width of 220 km (137 miles) makes the Rio de la Plata the widest river of the world.

The deepest river is the Kongo with a depth of up to 300 m (984 ft).

Chicago River has been colored green for St. Patrick's day.

Waterfalls

A waterfall is a place where water is at least partially free falling over a vertical drop or a series of steep drops in the course of a stream or river.

The highest waterfall is the Salto Ángel at 978 m in south-east Venezuela.

Mekong Falls in Laos (height of 21 m, 69 ft) is the widest (over 10 km, 6.2 miles) and with a current of 50,000 m³/s (13 million gallons/s) also the fall carrying the most water.

The largest curtain of water can be found at the Victoria Falls at the Zambesi River. The curtain is 1706 m wide and 99 m high (5,598 ft x 325 ft).

A rainbow forms in the spray of Victoria Falls.
Image: Joachim Huber

Water Content

The water content of humans diminishes from birth to death. A newborn consists of roughly 95% of water.
An old man only has 50%.

Meat contains 65% water.
A water melon is made up of 90% water.
A carrot contains 94%.
Butter 18%.

The salt water of Icelands Blue Lagoon comes from a 2000 m deep thermal well.

Source of Life

Evolution of life started in the water of the oceans. Today there is an estimated amount of 15 Million different life-forms on Earth. 51% of them are insects.

Most life-forms would perish without water.

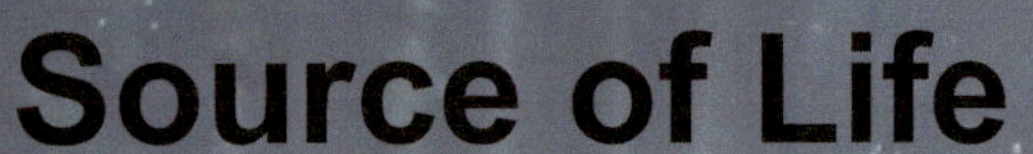

Australian Shepherd attempting to walk on water.

Water consumption

Every year 9,868,125 billion litres (2,606,882 billion gallons) of water are polluted. That amounts to 0.0007% of all water. .2% of all freshwater.

The average American uses 314 liters (83 gallons) of water each day. 24% are used for flushing the toilet, 20% in the shower, 19% in faucets, 17% by the cloth washer, 12% are lost through leaks.

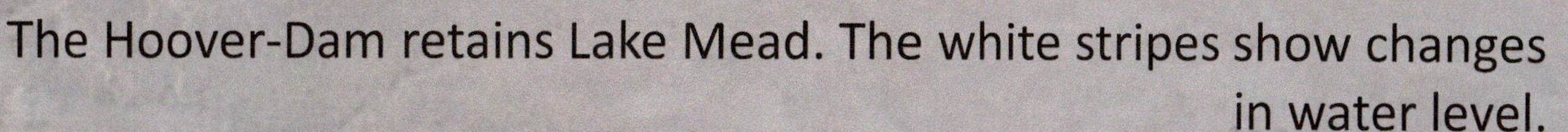

The Hoover-Dam retains Lake Mead. The white stripes show changes in water level.

Water of crystallization

Water can be loosely bound within other crystals.

Water of crystallization is discharged during heating. Burnt gypsum is free of water. Through addition of water gypsum hardens.

Cobalt-chloride enriched silica gel is blue if free of water of crystallization and becomes red through absorption of water.

The limestone terraces at Pamukkale in Turkey are deposits of warm spring water. Image: P. Vasiliadis

Autoprotolysis

Pure H_2O will inevitably split, to a small portion, into HO^- and H_3O^+ ions. These ions grant even pure water a small electric conductance.

Autoprotolysis is strongly dependent on temperature and influences the pH-Value.

At 0 °C (32 °F) the pH-Value is 7,47. At 100 °C (212 °F), it shifts towards 6,14, and the water becomes a acrid. At 25 °C (77 °F) the pH-Value is 7.

Devil's Bath at Wai-O-Tapu Thermal Wonderland on New Zealand's northern island is tainted green due to a high amount of sulphur.

Density Anomaly

The volume of a normal substance will increase with increasing temperature, and as the substance expands, the density is reduced. Hence a normal liquid would be warmest on top and coldest at the bottom.

Water is different. It reaches its highest density at 4 °C (39.2 °F). At 0°C (32 °F) the density suddenly drops and starts to increase with lower temperatures from thereon.

It is due to this anomaly that waters freezes from top to bottom. Lighter, colder water floats to the top while 4°C warm water sinks to the bottom.

Blue Lake in a extinct volcanic crater near Australia's Great Ocean Road changes its color each November from dark blue to turquoise.

Optical Transparency

Water has its highest transparency exactly in the area of the electromagnetic spectrum where the solar intensity is highest.

If this incredible coincidence did not exist, (if the water in our eyes was not transparent at these wavelengths), then we would not be able to see (or we would see much less).

Water is most transparent for blue light. This is also why it appears blue. Red and yellow colors of incoming light are absorbed more, hence most of the light reflected back to an observer is blue, giving deeper water its color.

A starfish takes a bath in the shallow waters of Coco Kay, Bahamas.

Surface Tension

Water has, next to Quicksilver, the highest surface tension of any liquid (72 mN/m at +20 °C) .

The high surface tension allows the formation of drops which is very important in the formation of rain.

It also grants some insects the power to walk on water.

Objects which should be drowning based on their density can remain afloat.

Mating water striders. Surface tension keeps them from drowning.
Image: Markus Gayda

Thermal Conductivity

Thermal conductivity describes the ability of a substance to conduct heat. It is measured in Watts per meter and Kelvin.

The thermal conductivity of water (0,56 W/m/K) is comparable with that of bricks, glass or polyethylene.

This low conductivity reduces the energy loss of humans, animals and plants. A resting human male looses 100 W to 200 W.

This river in Canterbury County on New Zealand's southern island is unbelievably blue.

Thermal Capacity

Thermal capacity describes the ability of a substance to store heat.

Water has the highest thermal capacity of all liquids. (4,18 kJ/kg/K at 20 °C). This makes water an excellent energy reservoir and coolant.

All nuclear power plants combined would need 500.000 years to increase the ocean's temperature by 1 °C.

The sun could do it in one year.

The Twelve Apostles consisted of nine limestone formations up to 60 m (197 ft) high at Australia's southern coast. Today only eight remain. The number 12 was a marketing decision!

Vaporization

Under normal pressure water will boil at 100 °C (212 °F) and start to vaporize.

Water has the highest specific Enthalpy of Evaporation of any known liquid (2453 kJ/kg at 20 °C).

Therefore water is the most suited liquid for transpiration in plants and perspiration in animals. This provides critical temperature management for plants, beasts and man.

A 75 kg (165 lbs) man can reduce his body temperature by .1 °C through evaporation of 100 ml (3.4 oz) of water.

Hot water evaporates from the Champagne Pool at New Zealand's northern Island. Orpiment (As_2S_3) and Stibnite (Sb_2S_3) sediments form a red rim.

Evaporization

Evaporization occurs in water below vaporization temperature, when the gas above the water is not yet saturated with water vapor.

Particles in gases, and in a similar fashion also in liquids, follow the Maxwell-Boltzmann-Distribution. This means, that there are faster and slower particles inside the gas and the liquid. Faster particles from the liquid can change into the gaseous state while slower particles from the gas become part of the liquid. Equilibrium is reached once these processes are occurring at the same rate.

For water this is the case when humidity reaches 100%.

The gypsum sand at White Sands National Monument in New Mexico is the remnant of a sea that evaporated 250 Million years ago.

Freezing Point

The Freezing Point describes the temperature at which water changes to ice. The normal freezing temperature of water is 0 °C (32 °F).

It is possible to reduce the Freezing Point through addition of salts. The lowest Freezing Point achieved in this fashion by Daniel Gabriel Fahrenheit (-17.8 °C, 0 °F) defines the zero point of the Fahrenheit scale.

A lack of condensation nuclei causes pure water to freeze not before reaching a temperature of -48,3 °C   (-55 °F). If the conditions are right a further cooling to -70 °C (-94 °F) is possible.

Tomb Raider, Beowulf & Grendel, Batman Begins and two James Bond movies were filmed at marvelous Jökulsárlón Lagoon.

Melting Point

The melting point describes the transition from ice to water. For pure water under normal pressure, this point defines the zero-point of the Celsius scale.

For regular substances the melting point will increase with increasing atmospheric pressure. The substance will remain solid up to higher temperatures. For water it is the other way around.

Strong magnetic fields can increase the melting point of water slightly.

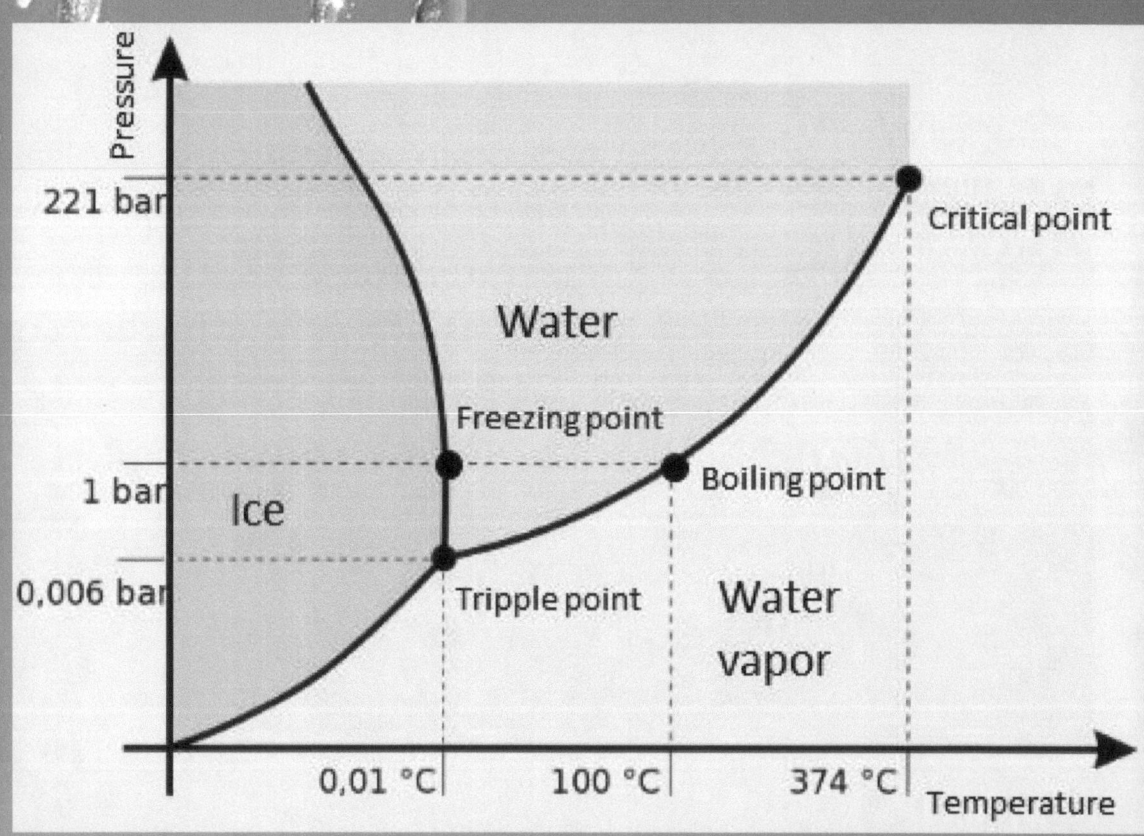

Simplified phase diagram of water. At the triple-point all states of matter coexist at the same time.

Mpemba Effect

Under certain circumstances warm water can freeze faster than cold water. For example 43°C warm water freezes in 206 minutes, while 19 °C cold water requires 280 minutes.

Despite the fact that the effect was already being discussed by Aristotle the reason of the phenomenon is still not completely understood.
Most likely a reduction of the amount of warm water through evaporization leads to a faster freezing of the remaining, smaller, amount of water.
There are no conclusive studies on other effects that may play a role.

Steam rises over Mammoth Hot Springs at Yellowstone National Park.
Image: Brocken Inaglory

Ice

Ice crystalizes in hexagonal structures to a transparent, colorless crystal. Ice is a mineral from the oxide group.

The phase diagram of Ice has more modifications than that of any other substance.

Ice with large amount of entrapped air bubbles is white. With declining amounts of inclusions ice will become greenish, blueish and ultimately transparent.

Ice can support the weight of a normal person starting at a thickness of 3".

Lake Fryxell can be found in the eastern parts of Antarctica between Canada- and Commonwealth Glacier. The lake was discovered by Sir Robert Falcon Scott. Image: Joe Mastroianni, NSF

Snow Crystals

Snow is created in the atmosphere at temperatures below -12 °C (10 °F) through accretion (growth or increase by the gradual accumulation of additional layers) of supercooled water molecules to a condensation nucleus. Water molecules combine at angles of exactly 60° or 120° which makes snow crystals perfect hexagons.

Temperature and humidity influence the appearance of snow crystals.

The chance of two snow crystals being identical is negligible. A single snow crystal includes about 10^{18} water molecules. This allows for more combinations than there are atoms in the universe.

From 1885 Wilson Bentley dedicated his life to the study of snow crystals. He documented over 5000 forms.
Image: Annick MONNIER, An-d

Snow Flakes

Snow crystals will become snow flakes. Light will be reflected by the different crystals in a diffuse fashion resulting in the white appearance of the snow flake.
Snow falls with a velocity of 4 km/h (2.5 mph) which is five times slower than rain.

A typical snow flake is roughly 5 mm (.2") in diameter. According to the Guinness Book of Records the largest snow flake documented was 38 cm (15") in diameter.

When a snow flake falls on water a high pitched sound can occur, which is unnoticeable to the human ear.

Snowfall at the Hofgarden in Düsseldorf. Chance of White Christmas in Düsseldorf is 23%. Image: Stöhrfall

Snow

Contrary to popular opinion the Eskimo do not have an extraordinary amount of words for snow.

Snow can be classified based on age, humidity, colour, density and origin.
The English language knows 26 words for snow on the ground. Examples include: Corn, Cornice, Crud, Crust, Depth hoar, Finger Drift, Firn, Champaign Powder, Slush, Snirt or Watermelon Snow.

At some point snow will be compressed under its own weight and ultimately become ice.

During snowmelt red algae color old snow reddish. Watermelon Snow is created. Image: Iwona Erskine-Kellie

Hail

Hailstones are clumps of ice with a diameter above 0.5 cm (.2"). Smaller clumps of ice are called Graupel or soft hail.

Hail occurs mainly during summer time. It is created in thunderclouds through condensation of supercooled water to ice.

The costliest hailstorm in US history amounted to 2 billion dollars in insured damages. It struck the I-70 corridor of eastern Kansas, across Missouri, into southwestern Illinois with baseball sized hails.

Large hail can reach up to 145 km/h (90 mph).

In 2010 a 875 g (1,92 lbs) hailstone with a diameter of 20 cm (7.9") was found in South Dakota.

Many small hailstones have formed a 6 cm (2.4") large specimen.
Image: NOAA

Clouds

Clouds are made of aerosols, small drops of water or ice crystals.

Clouds are not made of water vapor. As a gas the vapor stays invisible.

Mie-scattering of light and the Tyndall-Effect gives clouds their characteristic color.

In the Chilean town of Chungungo clouds are milked for water production.

Roll-Clouds, like here over Munich (Germany) are extremely rare to observe. The occur in conjunction with thunderstorms.

Fog

Cooling of humid air results in an over-saturation of water vapor and water droplets are formed.

Like in clouds these water droplets become visible through a combination of Mie-scattering and Tyndall Effect.

When this phenomenon occurs near the surface and visibility is reduced to 1 km or less it is called fog. If visibility is reduced below 200 m (656 ft), it is called heavy fog.

The layman can recognize fog if visibility is reduced below 350 m (1148 ft).

The space shuttle Challanger is moved through fog at Kennedy Space center towards the launch pad. Image: NASA

Rain

Rain is created in clouds from condensed water vapor.

Rain begins to fall when the ascending air currents in the clouds can no longer hold the water droplets in.

Average rainfall rate in the US varies from 9.5" (241 mm) in Nevada to 63.7" (1618 mm) in Hawaii.

Cherrapunji in India is the most rain-laden place on Earth with an average rainfall rate of 450" (11.439 mm).

Snapshot of rain-drops falling into a water puddle.

Rainbow

A rainbow can be observed if someone looks at a curtain of water droplets with the sun in with the sun at their back..

Within the water droplets light is refracted and reflected at the rear side of the drop. Refraction splits white light into the individual spectral colors. Simple reflection creates a rainbow at an angle of $42°$. Double reflection creates a second rainbow at $51°$. Both rainbows show each other their red color. In between the rainbows the sky is slightly darker.

Double rainbow is visible above the USS Arizona Memorial at Pearl Harbor.

Geysers

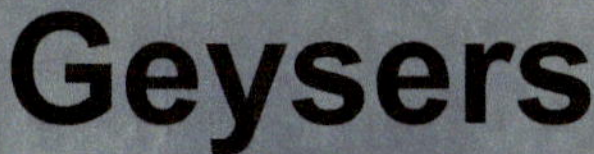

All Geysers are named after the Great Geyser on Iceland. Geysers are hot springs which erupt in a fountain of water in more or less regular intervals.

The most Geysers are located at Yellowstone National Park and in the Valley of Geysers in Russia.

One of the most reliable Geysers is Strokkur near the Great Geyser in Iceland. Strokkur erupts every 10 minutes.
The record for the highest eruption is held by Waimangu-Geysers in New Zealand (active between 1900 to 1904) with a height of 460 m.

Water rises from Geyser Strokkur seconds before the eruption.

Ebb and Flow

Falling tide (ebb) and rising tide (flow) switch every six hours.
The tide is high on the side facing the moon and facing away from the moon. Half way between the two the tide is low.
Tides are a result of the tidal force, which is the difference in gravitational force on the surface of the Earth compared to the Earth's center. The tidal force is directed away from the center.
At the open sea the moon rises the water level by 30 cm (11.8"). The contribution of the sun adds another 14 cm. (5.5")

Low tide at one of the D-Day beaches in Normandy where allied troops invaded Nazi Germany on June 6th 1944.

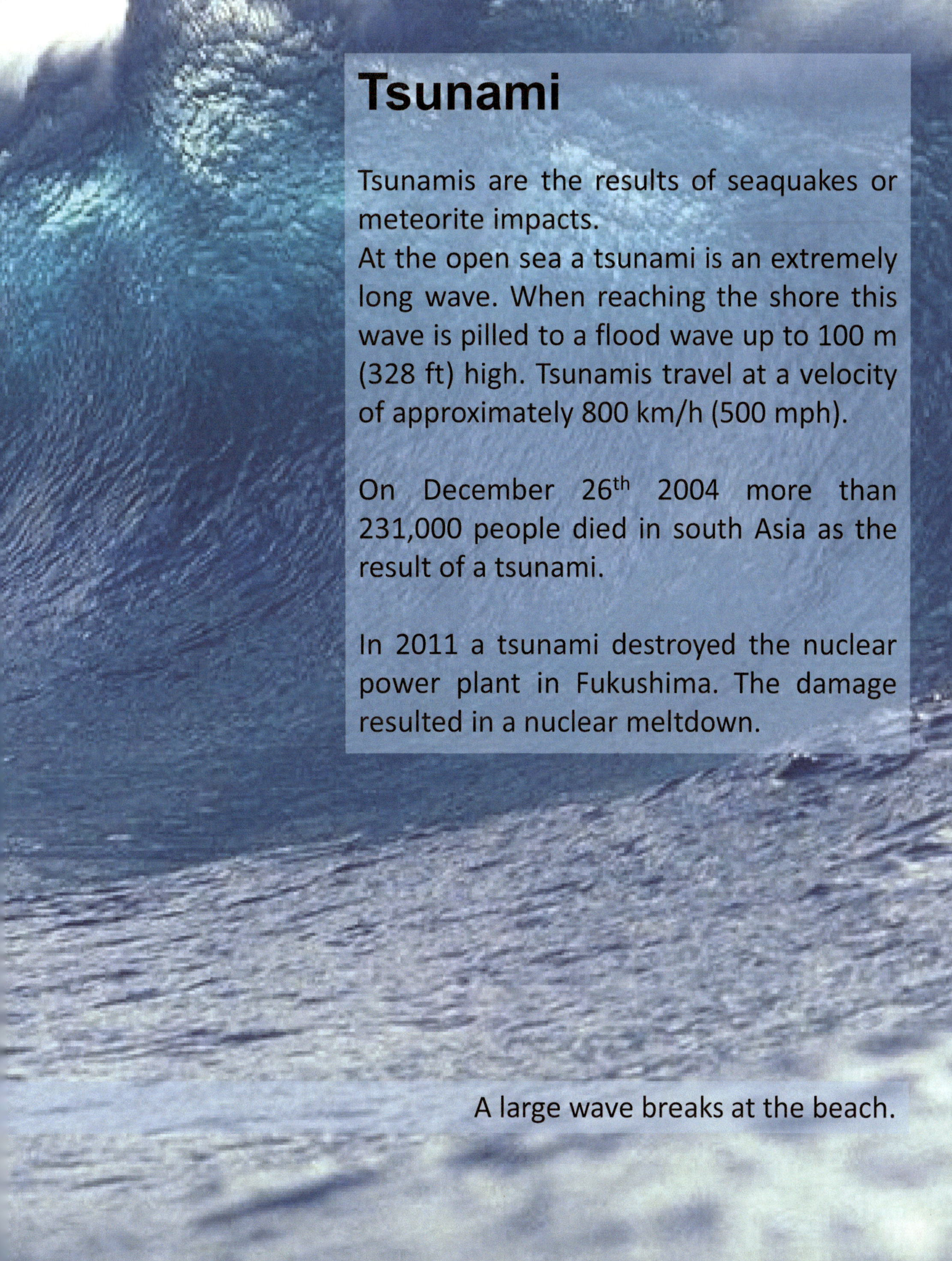

Tsunami

Tsunamis are the results of seaquakes or meteorite impacts.
At the open sea a tsunami is an extremely long wave. When reaching the shore this wave is pilled to a flood wave up to 100 m (328 ft) high. Tsunamis travel at a velocity of approximately 800 km/h (500 mph).

On December 26th 2004 more than 231,000 people died in south Asia as the result of a tsunami.

In 2011 a tsunami destroyed the nuclear power plant in Fukushima. The damage resulted in a nuclear meltdown.

A large wave breaks at the beach.

Water in the universe

Water is very common in the universe. Water vapor has been confirmed in galaxies which are up to 12 billion lightyears away.

Within the solar system water has mainly been found in the form of water ice on other planets and moons.

Our moon likely contains water in the craters of the polar regions. Mars contains large amounts of water ice below the surface.

Oceans of water are expected hidden beneath a crust of ice on some of the moons in the outer solar system.

Artists view of the quasar APM 08279+5255. Its water reservoir is estimated to exceed 100,000 solar masses. Image: NASA

Cryovulcanism

Cryovulcansim is an extraterrestrial form of vulcanism. A mixture of water and other volatile substances breaks through a curst of ice at temperatures below -150 °C. The discharged material freezes instantaneously and piles up to a volcano. The phenomenon has been observed on many icy moons in the outer solar system.

Image taken by the Cassini probe shows the eruption of a cryovulcano on Saturn's moon Enceladus.
Image: NASA/JPL/Space Science Institute

Image Credits

Title page, page 3-9, 11-17, 19-23, 31, 34-36 : Florian M. Nebel

Back page caution image credit: RTCNCA, https://commons.wikimedia.org/wiki/File:Caution_blank.svg, CC BY-SA 3.0

Page 2: http://commons.wikimedia.org/wiki/File:STS-95_Florida_From_Space.jpg, public domain

Page 10: http://commons.wikimedia.org/wiki/File:Victoria_Falls_%282541711854%29.jpg, CC BY-SA 2.0

Page 18: http://commons.wikimedia.org/wiki/File:Wasserl%C3%A4ufer_bei_der_Paarung_crop.jpg, CC BY-SA 3.0

Page 24: https://commons.wikimedia.org/wiki/File:Phasendiagramme.svg, public domain

https://commons.wikimedia.org/wiki/File:In_der_Sonne_schmelzende_Eiszapfen.JPG, public domain

Page 25: https://commons.wikimedia.org/wiki/File:Dead_trees_at_Mammoth_Hot_Springs.jpg, CC BY-SA 3.0

Page 26: https://commons.wikimedia.org/wiki/File:Fryxellsee_Opt.jpg, public domain

Page 27: http://commons.wikimedia.org/wiki/File:Fleur_de_givre_L3.jpg, CC BY-SA 3.0

Page 28: https://commons.wikimedia.org/wiki/File:D%C3%BCsseldorf_Hofgarten_2009.jpg, public domain

Page 29: http://commons.wikimedia.org/wiki/File:Snow_Algae_Textures.jpg, CC BY 2.0

Page 30: https://commons.wikimedia.org/wiki/File:Granizo.jpg, public domain

Page 32: http://commons.wikimedia.org/wiki/File:Space_Shuttle_Challenger_moving_through_fog.jpg, public domain

Page 33: http://pixabay.com/de/boot-regen-d%C3%BCster-schiff-wasser-507173/, CC0

Page 37: http://pixabay.com/de/welle-wasser-meer-tsunami-woge-11061/, CC0

Page 38: http://commons.wikimedia.org/wiki/File:Pamukkale_Hierapolis_Travertine_pools.JPG, CC BY-SA 3.0

Page 39: http://de.wikipedia.org/wiki/Wasservorkommen_im_Universum#mediaviewer/File:Black-hole-feeding-accreting-esa-nasa.jpg, public domain

Page 40: https://commons.wikimedia.org/wiki/File:Fountains_of_Enceladus_PIA07758.jpg, public domain

The original work has been modified.

Cover: A hump-back whale plays in the ocean off the coast of Maui.